AF483260

LIGHT AS AIR

A COLLECTION OF POEMS STEMMING FROM HEARTBREAK AND HEALING

CHANDINI KALYANARAMAN

Made with ❤ on the Notion Press Platform
www.notionpress.com

Contents

Preface *vii*

I. DESPAIR

1. A Basket 3
2. A Call Away 4
3. And They Say 6
4. Apathy 7
5. Bauble 8
6. Ditched Into Darkness 9
7. Go To Hell 10
8. His Absence 11
9. How Do You Win? 13
10. How Easy 14
11. Mom 15
12. My Frankenstein 16
13. Oh Uncle! 17
14. Over There 19
15. Radio 21
16. The Forgotten Vow 22
17. Together 23
18. Until 25
19. Loved And Lost 26
20. Another Mother 27
21. The End 28

Contents

II. AFFAIR

22. Her 33
23. Let's Go! 35
24. Look! 36
25. Morality 37
26. Stumbling Down 38
27. Tamed 40
28. The Artist 41
29. The Cuckold 43
30. The Goddess 44
31. Engulf In Flames 45

Contents

III. REPAIR

32. Blue 49

33. Rooted To Feel 50

34. I'm Okay 52

35. Jewellery 54

36. Liberty 55

37. Melancholy Strikes 56

38. Moment In The Future 58

39. Selenophile 59

40. She/Them 60

41. Trapped 61

42. In Love With Me 62

43. Love Is In The Air 63

44. What Doesn't Kill Me 64

45. Dedication 65

Author's Note 67

Preface

Marriage is hard. It is harder when it fails. It is only when one is at the end of the line does one realise, marriage does not have to be bigger than life, it is just a part of life. In the course of internalising and accepting a failed marriage, here is a collection of poems - stemming from understanding the descent of a marital relationship, the aftermath of separation, and the discovery of self-identity.

The poems in this book have been divided into three parts written over several years. The stage of Despair realised in a loveless marriage followed by the stage of affair, which describes exploration and sharing one's self with others for mutual companionship, and finally the stage of repair, a sacred stage of epiphany and fulfilment in independence (the strength that is discovered in being alone and embracing life as it is). Interspersed between these poems are musings that stand alone representing moments of radical emotions.

This book is not intended to hurt anyone. In fact, all relationships are beautiful in their own way, and here are penned thoughts denoting that building something from the heart is perfect in its own way and does not need to be moulded to societal dictations.

Here's to discovering various facets of yourself in the pages. I hope it leaves you a little healed as it did for me.

DESPAIR

I

1. A basket

He wove me a basket
basket of lies
Pretty... intricate little lies.
Layer after layer
A vessel filled with inauthenticity
That quenched my thirst.
For self-esteem
A search that began with him
And many others that followed.

Unveiling my temple
For anyone who would like to see
In denial that it was just me.
You're the prettiest of them all
That's not what I tell her
You're the fairest of them all
That's what I concur.
When all along, it was seesawing.
Our baggage we did carry
In that pretty little basket of lies.

2. A call away

The black screen in front of me
It makes my heart pound.
Just one text away,
Two strokes for a Hi is all it takes.
Yet, I cannot
The wall of pride is a hard one to break

Do you wonder
Where am I?
Am I fine
Or tearing up at thoughts of the decline
But you are a man
You wouldn't think twice.
Unless someday you turn back and feel
I missed that girl; she was nice.

That day, I would stare at the not-so-black screen.
No tear to cry
Reject the call
Begin to live a lie.
That I am fine indeed
Without you in my life.

Yet the pain you caused me
Will always reside.

3. And They Say

It's a match made in heaven, they say
It's all work and no play.
It gets better in time, they say.
I decay like flowers left outside on a sunny day.
Never leave the marriage bed, they say.
Could I lie in a pool of my own tears, rotting and hoping to fly away?
The grass is always greener, they say
I don't want to be single; I just want to be loved the right way,
There are plenty of fish in the sea, they say
I caught this one. Why can't I make him stay?
Men will be men, they say,
No matter what, he has to pay.
Time will heal all wounds, they say,
This excruciating pain should end someday, I pray.

4. Apathy

Tragedy struck once
Apathy, baby, show me some apathy.
Tragedy strikes again,
Apathy, I cannot refrain,
You lost your employment; you lost your loved one.
And I?
The dolphin was stuck in the cove,
There are no more tools in my kit to fix this.
My last nail was used for fixing the frames of my broken, numb heart
Iced, ice-cold, frozen.

Call it what you will.
Sympathy: I have nil
While you suffer silently.
I feel vehemently
That it did not get worse, and you have it so easy.
You would never come to me.
While I struggle with reality
Of having to make ends meet
Now, for both you and me.

5. Bauble

Eastward doth the wind blow.
Downward the sun doth glow
O'er the clearing, I sat
On the lush green grass mat.

Thoughts...
Foolish art thee, human being
Thou seeketh happiness in living.
Thy need is repentance for sins
Yet thou art cursed from birth.
Which begins,
A new era of one more soul that suffereth
The whips and scorns of time.
T'is, as one may say, is impossible
To be happy and to have suffer'd.

That this life is given by God to thee
It is absolutely nothing but a worthless bauble!

6. Ditched Into Darkness

The tragedy of loneliness.
Remembrance of a fond memory
Paralysed and faithless
Ditched into darkness.

I was so blind, so ignorant.
Four chambers are now filled,
Where 'twas empty; therein, sadness.

Arrogance in the first place,
Led to the utmost disgrace.
Trust beyond limitations

Resulting in this eternal pain.
Raindrops form at the corner of the eye when going away, apart.
There is no remedy other than love for a broken heart.

7. Go To Hell

Take your toxic masculinity,
And shove it where the sun doesn't shine.
This femme ain't buying what you're selling
This world without you will do just fine.
And when you start spewing hatred
It's a whole lot of ignorance.
The talons you try to clutch with,
It cannot capture this fire of resistance.
You may drop your words now,
But wounds will not leave, no matter how.
So go ahead and take your cheapest shot,
You may strike when the iron is hot
Yet this Phoenix will rise
From the ashes again when you least expect.

8. His absence

Where there were his lifelines on mine,
The palm stays empty, with just a pen left behind.
Where there was no space between unification
There's now distance and a fleeting sensation

One can sit and wonder... What sin brought on this despair?
Those eyes that I no longer see, those lips I no longer taste, those fingers I no longer feel,
Is it all fair?

We used to lie with our heartbeats combined
As rhythmic snores played a lullaby to my ears
This separation was determined,
Doubt playing with my fears
He seemed to have that aura, that power.
That falling rain and that tree under which I cower,
Now my forest lies bare…
Waiting for him to recover

The materialisation of a relation on the horizon.
It is too far away to reach, just plain agonising
In an ocean of tears, this love boat is capsizing.

Like sweeping blood off a rusted sword
Or separating the ink from the paper within the written word.
A part of me is with you and will not let me leave
And part of you is with me and won't let me be.

9. How Do You Win?

My mouth moves
And he scrolls
Words are lost in sound; for him, words are lost in text.
The game is rigged, you may think,
To whose gain?
The cards are dealt
Yet nobody gets the pot.
One spouse lost without purpose,
One spouse lost in ignorance
It's cold outside, and the body aches.
Homesickness for a nomad may be fake
At some point, longing comes to an end
You surrender to the winner who never played the game.

10. How Easy

The spinning fan beckons.
A spineless me
How easy is that full stop at the end of the sente…?
Hence, it trails off
Screams of invites fill the hell below,
On the above, an unreachable heaven aglow.
I stare into the amber lamp
Wondering if this would be the perfect moment to say goodbye
A slit... a noose... a pen in the end is all I have.
Oh, the irony.
As they say, those who raise the sword will die by it.
As will those who raise the pen... isn't it?

11. Mom

Mama, where does your deepest faith lie?
By the crushed petals at the inanimate idol's feet,
Or in the consciousness that lives and thrives.

Mama, where does your line of duty end?
In the thread of the man who possesses you,
Or from the womb that came the being, a facsimile.

Mama, what is the extent of your tolerance?
Reproach me once again,
Say I have to stay in spite of the pain.

Mama, tell me how to keep a man?
Submit grudgingly as you did
My wants and needs are forever hidden.

Mama, show me the way out, can you?
Or do years of conditioning by your parents subdue you?
Just like your conditioning leaves me with a rue
With no way out and no clue
I wither like a daisy without the dew.

12. My Frankenstein

The monster of Frankenstein is real.
It resides within me…
The power of a thousand volts of electricity
Out to shock anyone who dares reach out.
Pieces of rotting flesh stitched together by strings,
Eyes that see no kindness, lips that speak of no love, and hands that grasp no affection between them.
I live like a corpse,
With each passing day, I wake
Death walks among us.
Stemming from a heart turned black as a stone
Out to collect more broken hearts
I move forward, forever alone.

13. Oh Uncle!

I heard you had passed away,
A doll is what I have in my memory
An offer in the past that I couldn't refuse.
Yet you have now refused to say goodbye,
Why?

I wonder…
Are you looking down?
Have I bloomed? Am I lovely now?
Do you see similarities with me?
Teardrop after teardrop,
Remembering the butterflies on the wall,
That's what you are... winged in white.

A veena plays in the background,
I remember,
The striped tees you wore matched the grey strands on your black head.
2 years! Two years since you died. So absquatulate,
I was told of your death only yesterday.

Was it the floods? Was it my failing marriage? Was it your isolation?

Did you go out on a peak? Was it a high point of your life?
Or were you dragged across the streets? Alone… in the lack of a sire or wife.
Was it in a van? Decorated with flowers?
Are you under the soil or in a bowl as ashes?
Dust settles either way in the end.

Not to me.
I still seek, I search, I hope,
Did you leave me anything? A note?
Maybe I am not all cried out.
Maybe I don't understand.
Maybe I should hold on to hope.
Maybe you could still bless me; maybe I shouldn't mope.

But wherever you are, whether you are here or if you did die,
This is my final chance to say goodbye.

14. Over There

That's where I studied, played, and lived.
I point
To a place that feels alien now.

Lifted out of my own skin.
In a city that I have to share with you.
A bleak future is all I see.
All that's left.

No warm lips on mine.
Just the desire to leave.
To mend my broken heart
And heal it atop snow-capped peaks.

Away from what used to be home.
Built with you.
But you baby,
You've won!

Take it all away
My 360-degree comfort
The view from my window.
The dark cat is by my feet.

Take it all silently.
Maybe someday I will turn back and see.
It was never meant to be.
But now,
Loneliness is all I have with me.

15. Radio

Under the city lights.
On the way to the party,
In the cab, they sat seething and fuming
until the radio turned on.
and blending with traffic sirens, played
'Nothing's gonna change my love for you'
They said nothing and just held hands.
Silently smiling, looking out the window.

16. The Forgotten Vow

I, Husband, take thee, wife.
And vow to kiss you before I leave every room,
Follow and support every passion you have.
Be with you in person or virtually during rainy days,
Bring your ice cream on special days,
make love to you regardless of your body changes,
Laugh at inside jokes even amidst company,
and forever let you grow at your own pace.

17. Together

There is a bird at our window pecking on nothing.
Revel in that sentence for a minute.
In this home, I built with you.
Filled with our imprints.
Every nook and every corner.
The home is like our bodies
I know it all like the back of my hand.
It begs for all types of reconciliation.
But none of them land.

Is it familiarity? Is it conditioning?
Is there really no chance of escaping?
Alcohol plays the cure when I consume.
But then it shuts you down, I assume.

They said marriage is a compromise.
They said it is companionship.
Problems will arise,
Yet you will be joined at the hip

Nobody says marriage won't give you
What you do not possess.
If you do not see eye to eye.

You will not progress.
This home that we lived in as friends, then roommates, and now merely shadows.
It is a testament to the nothing that the bird on the window is now pecking at.

18. Until

There were no candlelit dinners
No blood-red roses.
A meme shared was a moment shared
There were no gifts.
No songs were dedicated.
A life was changed when rings were exchanged
The families gave them 20 minutes to talk.
She told him she hated going to bed with unresolved fights.
Ever since then, it has always been sleepless nights.
Fast forward a decade, and she never got what she asked for.
A divorce isn't that hard to grant after 10 years have passed.
Until one fateful day when she decided,
To get him drunk, to make him see,
Getting rid of him is the only way for her to be free.
It was over soon, and he was gone,
But the pain never left.
Literally, the ghostly grip on her neck will always be felt!

19. Loved and Lost

To the person who said:
It is better to have loved and lost
Then never to have loved at all
You did not love enough.
To lose yourself
For it is better not to have loved
Than to lose your life
Over the one you loved.

20. Another Mother

I always wondered why the suffix was called 'in-law'?
Would the law ensure you cared?
Or would law ask you to beware?

You bore him in your womb,
I bore him on my back.
Gave him what you did for half of your life
All because I was called the wife.

Stepping into the role as if I were tailor-made for it
Making decisions as I deemed fit.
Yet you hovered, huffed, and puffed
Destroyed our home in a gruff.

You were near the competition.
To relinquish control, I understand the hesitation,
But know this, that just as you were once a princess to your father.
I too was a little girl that you are now hell-bent to bother.

21. The End

There are signs when it is the end.
There is a science behind the end.
When words fail you both,
Silence falls as easily as spring water from a mountain glacier.
A pandemic that led to avoidance room to room,
He was once my groom.

There are signs when it is the end,
The bed is so inviting,
Paper sheets beckon you to write goodbye letters,
No tomorrows found at the bottom of the bottle.
The promise of silence with a purpose.
This end in the end is better, I suppose.

AFFAIR

II

22. Her

Her ruby-red lips stand out under the neon light.
I grab the drink in my hand, my grip trembling, realising how hooked I am,
Does she want this as much as I do?
Do I have her consent? Does she want me too?

I have not felt this way in a long time.
In anger, I had sworn off men in line.
Now my eyes notice them all.
Pronouns no longer stand tall.

An ally I will always be.
But tonight, on an experiment that will shake the foundation of me.
It is not the gender I see.
Through the lens of inclusivity.
I discover a whole new spectrum in my destiny.

Would her touch be soft? Would his be rough?
Is the stereotype too much?
Shun away from what history has taught us
Traits make a person, not the faces.

I am on a new journey, ferrying these partners across the perils.
To a side where there is pure bliss.
If someone saw, at the corner of their eye, would they fuss?
I don't care. I am the reformed icon of love. I am Venus!

23. Let's Go!

Let's go away, darling. Go to Goa, drink by the ocean,
listen to nature amongst shells,
let the wind rustle our hair.
Eat till we can't breathe, be loud,
dance till our calves hurt,
ride till our fuel runs dry, and then maybe
come back home to our unaware spouses.

24. Look!

When they were done making love, he fell deeply asleep in her arms.

She turned around and whispered in his ear just before drifting off.

"Honey, look! I am healing."

25. Morality

Morality and mortality cannot go hand in hand.
When you know you will be gone soon, wouldn't you live the best you ever can?
Call me pretty; call me the fairest in the land.
Absolute surrender is what I demand.

The toys lay bare by the nightstand.
Ready to put on a show on command
This is what carnality looks like first-hand.
No holds are barred; act like you are unmanned.

After all, manners are only for the bland.
But we, my dear, are the new brand.
So come over, let's hang.
I promise to make you go, "Oh, damn!"

26. Stumbling Down

I stumbled across him when I was lost in a way.
He was no angel; hell wasn't built in a day.
His eyes bore through my soul.
It made me feel like I was the only girl in the world.
He whispered sweet nothings, and I was shaken.
From the tip of my fingertips to the depth of my innards, I was hooked.

He touched me slightly, lips parted, breathing down my neck.
And in that sweet agony, I forgot myself.
His ghoulish frame is a silhouette of a thousand stars.
Each drowning me in desire is like a black hole.
He was by my side, behind, all around me.
Like being caressed by the waves of a tidal sea.

Hunger knew no bounds.
Yet each time you fed the beast, it came back for another round.
We belonged to no one: children of the night.
But when it entwined, I was his, and he was mine.

He whispered, "Do you think you could fall in the name of a memory?"
And I wondered if I would have the courage to say one day, "This wildness is just not me."

27. Tamed

My Femininity,
It is tamed once again.
In the past, the beholder of
My anatomy's blueprint,
A long while ago, but now
Tamed by whose smile I falter.
These are affairs of the mind.
I stopped if only it were not for the ink across my heart spelling the former's name.
The work spouse is nescient,
While the ball and chain hang heavy
Throughout the stroll
To walk of shame.
I am torn between... like a she-canine with two masters,
A child playing at the mouth of a lion's den,
Come, let's open the Pandora's box.
Forget the marital vows.
But it is not-so-black and white; shades of grey everywhere.
The graph is filled with struggles, and the median is happiness.
Yet, I will not step out. I am bound by the ethics of it all!

28. The Artist

Every time he makes love to me, it's art.
The frame of the bed is where the painting lies
Us, intertwined in a celestial silhouette.
Every touch of his is a stroke of paint…

I turn crimson red, like a moon that is impacted by the various ambers of the sun's rays touched by a million hands.
His beard, a brush... creating lines of passion across my plain skin.

The palate of his lips leaves tiny ripples all over the landscape.
Roses wherever he touches.
As his lips make rainbows out of my ribs.

I think of Da Vinci, of Van Gogh, and of the love I hold in my arms.
Maybe the greatest of them all?
A painter beyond the test of time…
Sketching, etching memories that will last forever.

He draws all night, well into the dawn, as I cry at the resulting perfection!
A thousand trips to the heaven within me,
And I wonder... am I the artist, or is he?

29. The Cuckold

The cuckold does not know.
About another's attentive stare
The cuckold does not know
About thoughts laid bare
The cuckold does not know
Nor does he care

The cuckold cannot see.
What's plain in front of he
The cuckold cannot see.
How much is it affecting me?
The cuckold cannot see.
What can finally set me free?

The cuckold tries
Maybe I can too
The cuckold cries
So I let him woo
The cuckold begs
But he still does not have a clue.
The cuckold hopes
The extinguished fire would burn again.

30. The Goddess

In the depth between her legs.
There lay a spot of paradise.
Where he does many a pit-stop
Each visit is a pilgrimage.
Although the Goddess would beg him to stay
In heaven for eternity,
The wanderer never could.
For He had other Gods to slay.

31. Engulf in flames

Spread your wings
In the name of love.
And fly into me
I will engulf you
In the flames of my desire,
And set your soul on fire.

Like a warm, gooey chocolate cake,
That crumbles in every bite,
So comfortable are your arms tonight.

In the morning, leave without saying goodbye,
To see you walk away, I would much rather die.

REPAIR

32. Blue

Is the colour blue really blue?
Or is what I see as blue what you do, too?
When colours do not have guarantees.
And when it relies heavily on witness pleas.
If one cannot define the colour blue,
Whether you tried hard enough, do you have a clue?

We reach back, our minds elastic.
Wondering if we gave it our best.
When the answer is chaotic,
Our minds are never laid to rest.
Digging deep into the magical Pensieve
Moments that you want to retrieve.
Wondering if you had played it differently.
Would the results be aligned perfectly?

Nothing is what it seems.
One could dream; one could scheme.
The ramifications are unworthy
When our understanding of blue is murky,
Stay still, beating heart.
It's the best way to set it free.

33. Rooted to feel

If I were to plant
A new sensation
In the ground, amidst the ashes.
Of our once-burning passion
Can love sustain and grow?

I wish you well,
Be at peace, never dismay.
You deserve it all
With a pinch of problems, that's all.

I regret not the days of the past.
Just the youth I lost.
Sitting in the same place.
Waiting for a sunny day.
Like a house plant
But at what cost?

Grow where you are
Or travel afar
Nourish on conversations.
Invest in others' emotions

Realise that love usually grows in an unlikely place.
It will come to you when you give up the chase.

34. I'm Okay

I spot,
The tears are going down the drain.
They're different from the water.
Encapsulated in silver.
The lining of hope.

The feline on my lap.
Breathing life into my veins.
As we watch the sunrise.
Between the rains

When songs lose all meaning.
The wind stops singing.
The grass seems greener there, far away.
Reaching it is tough; walk away.

Spirit flutters, flying over the blue rooftops.
Gaze at the horizon
Maybe the taste will come back.
A gourmet for life.

Matchbox square windows.
Of the soul

Doves visit
Bring a symbol of hope.
Come in, for there's plenty of love to give and losses to mope.

35. Jewellery

The sounds of the wedding march play in a distant corner
Filling the room as I looked at the reflection in the mirror.
In front of me is a set of amethyst accessories,
Even the most expensive will not appease.
The apprehensions of a bride on the day
Cold feet are an understatement, one could say.
Wearing stones and metals of the earth had no appeal,
My displeasure, meagre shine won't conceal

Adorned in the finest, I reach the altar.
A guillotine made of mortar.
Another added to the collection.
The ring on my finger.
Now, I am set to change my life.

Half a decade passes before I see them again.
Hidden away in a velvet pouch with no one to maintain
I must return them to where they belong.
They were never mine; never did I long
Beautiful jewellery, a reminder of a memory that has passed
That all things, no matter how precious, will never last.

36. Liberty

The petal of the sunflower licks my cheek
I remember the day when I burnt my finger on the kettle's spout

The snow-capped mountains fill my sight.
I remember when hosting extended family was my plight.

The sweetened raindrops kiss my forehead.
I remember when I lay for hours, waiting alone in bed.

The soft, velvety grass caresses my feet
I remember when endless arguments had me beaten.

The river streams are cool to the touch.
I remember waiting for the love that I missed so much.

The crisp light air fills my insides
I remember no more as I walked out of the tent in a glorious stride.

37. Melancholy Strikes

Melancholy strikes...
When the city seems alien to you.
The streets lead to nowhere; the lights seem to say farewell.
When the brewed English tea runs cold,
The flowers are withered, and the garden is dull beneath the grey, cloudy skies.

When long drives with deep conversations are what you hoped for.
But you are here just driving over a precipice to the rocks below.
Because leaps of faith never work,
No one will catch you.

When the town is dark,
Your once rose-tinted lens is covered in soot.
From ashes of burnt dreams.

When Pavlov seems like a genius,
What a terrible habit it is to believe and be lied to.

When that framed photo screams deception,
One-arm distance relationships that never finish the course.
You run with all your might, but each obstacle cuts short your reality.
When the sea's waves bleed onto the shore, ink bleeds onto paper.
When Melancholy strikes, it consumes.
Ignites and fervently changes the heart cocooned in intense fervour.

38. Moment in the Future

This July, I saw him again
The sun shone through the gap between the branches
illuminating the hand he was holding - hers.
I smiled and walked away,
Glad he took my advice in the end.

39. Selenophile

Aglow in perfection
Forever in love with the sun.

I try to capture her
Between my thumb and finger.
The Alluring will always be eluding
Unimaginably larger
Then, the picture caught on the screen.

Irrevocably captivating
She graces every windowsill
Like people's royalty

Named after her
I bathe in her luminescence
The clouds' part like dropped pearls
A baroque to behold!

Come home, she cries
The rays extended like ropes.
Maybe... Some day?
When I'm finally at peace, I reply.

40. She/Them

We were all bound by the same organ
A bond that arises out of understanding
A gendered community of sorts
We are now joined in a sisterhood
Against the one who hurt one of us.
They stand tall next to me
A dance that one does around the Maypole
They are around me, encouraging me, empowering me
They state the rules,
A way to move forward
A cosmopolitan, a road trip, some spill sessions
They hold my hand, their faces aglow with awareness,
Having been on the same path as me
Where they will stray again, and I would do the ritual.
Encouraging and empowering
Their laughter is a healing sound to the soul
An eternal moment now prescribed
As I start again on the onward journey
My sisters will be there for me.

41. Trapped

If I were stuck in the crevices of love,
Could I amputate my heart to survive you?

If I were in love and I knew it
Could I pass it off as a dream or an illusion, as I see fit?

Like the painting of Damayanthi waiting on Nala's promise.
My heart is frozen on this paper; only with your presence is there any solace.

42. In love with me

To fall in love with myself.
Over and over again
Is the same feeling as discovering
New happiness in little moments.
Again, and again.

43. Love is in the Air

When in love with life,
Love is in the air.
It is in the first bite of that sweet cheesecake,
It is in the petals of that single rose,
It is in the green of the succulent you grow by your desk.

Love is indefinite
It is neither a glorious nor a tragic story.
It makes you wonder; it makes you surrender
It is fluid and unconventional.
At the same time scandalous and controversial!

Love is limitless
You have enough for yourself.
And more to give to others
It spills over, touching everything in its way like lava.
It is in the number of people you meet over your lifetime,
It is present in every smile, every act of kindness, and every possibility.

44. What doesn't kill me

What doesn't kill me,
Makes me bleed in words,
Makes me wince in pain,
Makes cry in agony
Moulds me into a shape like ebony,
Makes me learn a lesson
A hundred philosophers couldn't teach.
That the power lies in me,
To push myself and reach.
It chisels away the fear
Of being alone,
Makes me gain peace
And confidence to be airborne.
What doesn't kill me is no longer vague
It is the end of the line in love
From which there is always an escape.

45. Dedication

Somewhere over the rainbow,
A place where time stands still
Nostalgia will drown you
The memory of a lost love will burn through.
Hope in the things unseen and hold your faith,
Onwards shall we go, attempting,
Stepping on the same path one last time
Halfway there, my love.

Author's Note

Thank you for purchasing this book. The raw emotions exposed in this book are a culmination of a turbulent decade and do not intend to hurt anyone I know. As a reader/rider of the book, I hope you discovered a new spectrum of possibilities within you to feel, after going through my emotional rollercoaster. I truly wish you find the peace to alter or revel in the type of relationship you have or hope would come to you. Remember all relationships are successful for they make us happy or expose our innermost feelings.

At this juncture, I want to thank everyone who has been a friend, a fleeting comment, a thoughtful colleague, or simply part of a fading memory, be it painful or joyous. I would like to thank my previous partner for being a good person and taking it all in stride. I thank my lifelong friends who are always in my mind and me in theirs, even if not in talking terms, and my parents who give me plenty of material to write on. I also want to take a moment to thank my friends from the Toastmasters International fraternity.

Follow Me For More On Instagram

CHANDINIKALYANARAMAN

www.ingramcontent.com/pod-product-compliance
Lightning Source LLC
Chambersburg PA
CBHW030858120726
48008CB00002B/32
9798896324188